IMAGES
of America

NATCHITOCHES

Cammie Henry, seen in her restored gardens at Melrose, preserved the great history of Melrose, Natchitoches Parish, and Louisiana through hundreds of scrapbooks. Those scrapbooks are now housed at the Cammie G. Henry Research Center at the Watson Memorial Library on the campus of Northwestern State University. Many of the photographs contained in this book were preserved by Cammie Henry.

IMAGES
of America

NATCHITOCHES

The Joyous Coast Foundation

ARCADIA
PUBLISHING

Published by Arcadia Publishing
Charleston, South Carolina

Library of Congress Catalog Card Number: 2002116280

For all general information contact Arcadia Publishing at:
Telephone 843-853-2070
Fax 843-853-0044
E-mail sales@arcadiapublishing.com
For customer service and orders:
Toll-Free 1-888-313-2665

Visit us on the Internet at www.arcadiapublishing.com

The Guy House was built by Samuel Eldridge Guy c. 1850. It is a Greek Revival house that was located in a pasture five miles south of Mansfield and two miles south of the Battle of Mansfield. In 2002, the house was moved by the Joyous Coast Foundation to Natchitoches, where it is presently being restored. It is now located at 309 Rue Pine.

CONTENTS

Marcotte's Map of Cane River and Natchitoches was printed in 1845. The map indicates all the colonial trails and rivers used by the French and Native Americans prior to the Louisiana Purchase. Marcotte was a map making company in the New Orleans Vieux Carre and was only in existence for two years.

ACKNOWLEDGMENTS

On behalf of The Joyous Coast Foundation, L.L.C., I would like to express my sincere gratitude to the following individuals for their assistance in helping me comprise this historical book on Natchitoches: Iris Harper, Lanie Adkins, and Denise O'Bannon at the Natchitoches Tourist Commission for providing me with photographs of the Christmas lights and festival; Stephanie Masson and Leah Jackson at *The Natchitoches Times* for providing me with information and photographs on several of the houses and people included in the book; my secretaries, Leigh, Shuanna, Tricia, and Robbie, for the numerous errands they ran for me; my wife, Bridget, for her support and for allowing me to use our home computer to prepare the text of the book; and Kelle Broome, my editor at Arcadia, for her patience and guidance.

Lastly, I would like to thank Mary Linn Wernet and the staff of the Cammie G. Henry Research Center for their assistance and for allowing me to use the wonderful resources of the research center. Included in the book are photographs from several collections housed at the center, including the Cammie G. Henry, Giles W. Milspaugh Jr., Robert "Bobby" DeBlieux, Curtis Guillet, B.A. Cohen, Arthur Babb, Mrs. J. Alphonse Prud'homme, George Williamson, Tommy Johnson, and Caroline Dormon collections. I would especially like to thank Sonny Carter for his guidance on the selection of photographs and for the many hours he spent scanning many of the images included in the book. My sincere appreciation goes to Robert "Bobby" DeBlieux for providing me with numerous materials that I used in comprising the histories of many of the homes, plantations, and buildings depicted in the book. One reason Natchitoches is such a special place is because people like Bobby had the vision to preserve the unique and wonderful culture and history of Natchitoches Parish.

The Joyous Coast Foundation, L.L.C. was founded in 2002 as a historic preservation group. Its founding members are Tom Paquette, Aaron Savoie, Ben Fidelak, Keri Fidelak, and Payne Williams. *Images of America: Natchitoches* is the second project of the Joyous Coast Foundation. Its first project was the movement of the Guy House from Mansfield, Louisiana to Natchitoches. The Guy House is presently being restored and preserved for future generations.

INTRODUCTION

Natchitoches is the oldest permanent settlement in the Louisiana Purchase. It was founded in 1714 by a French Canadian, Louis Juchereau de St. Denis. St. Denis was en route to Mexico from Mobile, Alabama on a trade mission when he stopped in an area occupied by the Natchitoches Indians. He constructed two huts in the village and left a detachment to trade with the Native Americans. In 1716, Sieur Charles Claude Dutisne was sent to Natchitoches to construct a fort to prevent further Spanish expansion in the new world. Erected on a hill overlooking what is today Cane River Lake, the fort was named Fort St. Jean Baptiste. Natchitoches became the westernmost outpost of the French Colonial Empire in the West.

The name Natchitoches ("Nak-a-tish") was taken from the Natchitoches Indian tribe, which was part of the Caddo Confederation, who lived in the area that now comprises Natchitoches Parish. After Fort St. Jean Baptiste was erected, the French post prospered through illegal trade with the Spanish at Los Adaes and St. Denis's significant ties to the Native American tribes throughout the area. It was through these ties that he was able to stop the Natchez Indian invasion of Fort St. Jean Baptiste in 1731. The fort continued to prosper even after St. Denis's death in 1744. St. Denis's son-in-law, Jean Louis Caesar deBlanc deNeuveville, served as commandant of Fort St. Jean Baptiste until Spain took over the fort at the end of the French-Indian War in 1763.

The Spanish commandant, Christophe Athanase Fortunat de Mezieres, was St. Denis's son-in-law and had been appointed governor of Texas. During Spanish rule, the fort became one of many small settlements in Spanish North America and began to decline. One significant event during Spanish rule was that the inhabitants of Natchitoches began to move away from the fort and into the downtown area, where they built homes and shops along what is now Rue Front.

In 1803, the United States and France entered into the Louisiana Purchase and Natchitoches was once again subjected to another cultural influence. Soon after, a border war between Spain and the United States erupted over the Texas/Louisiana border. In 1806, Gen. James Wilkerson and the United States army entered Natchitoches. Wilkerson later met with Spanish lieutenant colonel Simon de Hervera and an agreement was reached through the Neutral Ground Treaty. The border dispute was eventually settled years later through the Adams-Onis Treaty. Natchitoches continued to grow, but tragedies occurred in 1823 and 1838 when the Church of St. Francis burned along with numerous homes, houses, and buildings in the downtown area.

Through the Antebellum period, Natchitoches and the Cane River plantations became a thriving area. Natchitoches received steamboat service from New Orleans as early as 1820. Natchitoches also benefited by the log jam, called the Great Raft, which blocked further travel upstream from Natchitoches. In 1832, Captain Shreve was appointed Superintendent of the Western River Improvements by Vice President John C. Calhoun. Over time, as the log jam was slowly removed, the flow of the Red River shifted from the Cane River channel to Grand Ecore. Thus, Natchitoches was assessable to steamboat traffic at only certain times of the year. By 1838, nearly all river traffic had bypassed Natchitoches and immensely curtailed the town's growth.

The town of Natchitoches was greatly spared during the Civil War. In 1864, Union general Nathaniel Banks was defeated at the Battles of Mansfield and Pleasant Hill. During the Union army's retreat, the divisions of General Banks and Union general A.J. Smith occupied Natchitoches. It was feared that Natchitoches, like many other Southern towns, would be burned by Union troops. However, it is believed that through intervention from Bishop Martin and through the friendships that several Natchitoches residents had with Gen. U.S. Grant, the town of Natchitoches was spared. At the end of the Civil War, all of the plantations on the east side of Cane River had been burned with the exception of Melrose Plantation, which was then called Yucca Plantation. In addition, many other Natchitoches stores and buildings had been burned and their goods destroyed or stolen.

Natchitoches slowly attempted to rebuild its economy after the Civil War. It suffered another setback when the Texas and Pacific Railroad bypassed Natchitoches for Cypress. It was not until the building of the Natchitoches Land and Railroad Company that the city's economic fortunes rebounded and resulted in a building boom. Natchitoches was also boosted economically in 1884 with the founding of the Louisiana State Normal School. This university, which is now known as Northwestern State University, still exists and is prospering today.

The 20th century brought great progress to Natchitoches. The town's economy diversified to include numerous businesses. Natchitoches has also received national exposure through several movies, including *Steel Magnolias*, which was written by Natchitoches native Robert Harling and was filmed in Natchitoches in 1988. In 1990, *The Man in the Moon*, which starred Reese Witherspoon and Sam Waterson, was also filmed in Natchitoches Parish. These movies along with the renewed interest in the National Landmark Historic District created a boom in tourism, displayed through a prosperous bed and breakfast industry and a dramatic increase in the number of tourists who visit Natchitoches each year. The tourist trade will also receive a tremendous boost in 2004 with the opening of the Cane River Creole National Park and the Cane River National Heritage Area.

Natchitoches Parish is the heart of a unique area referred to as the Cane River Country. Its origins include a mixture of cultures, including European, African, Native American, French Creole, and Spanish, which have lived in Natchitoches Parish for the past 300 years. This unique and diverse area continues to prosper today and offers a glimpse of how a myriad of cultures can come together to create a historic and cultural paradise.

One

COLONIAL
NATCHITOCHES

This is bust of Louis Juchereau de St. Denis, the founder of Natchitoches. St. Denis first met the Natchitoches Indians in 1701. In 1705, when flooding from the Red River had destroyed their crops, St. Denis invited the Natchitoches tribe to move to an area he controlled near Lake Pontchartrain. In return for his kindness, St. Denis received tattoos from the tribe that allowed him to cultivate strong trade ties and summon numerous Indian warriors in times of need.

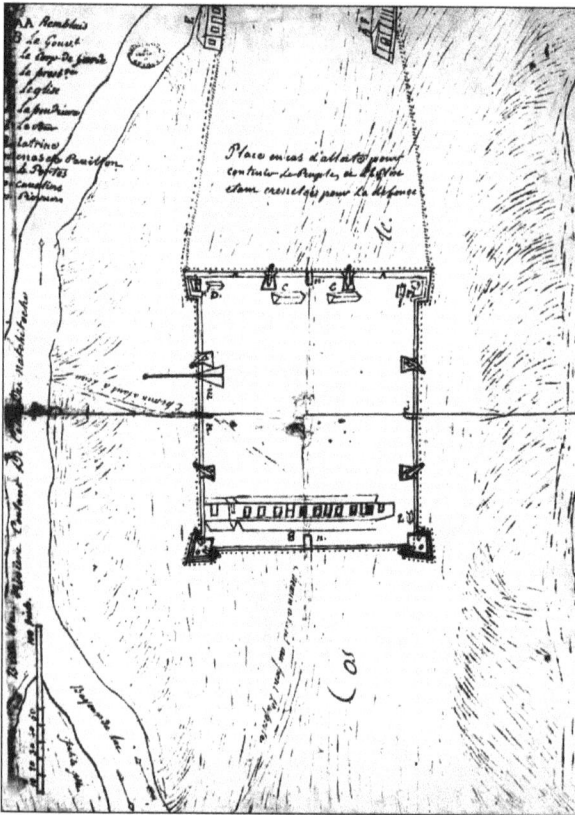

The first Fort St. Jean Baptiste was erected in 1716 and later burned in the early 1730s. It was moved to the present-day American Cemetery and a second fort was erected in 1737. The fort was taken over by Spanish governor Ulloa in 1766 and was again transferred to France and eventually the United States as part of the Louisiana Purchase in 1803.

A replica of the fort can now be seen as part of the Louisiana State Parks Commemorative Area. The fort is located at 130 Rue Moreau.

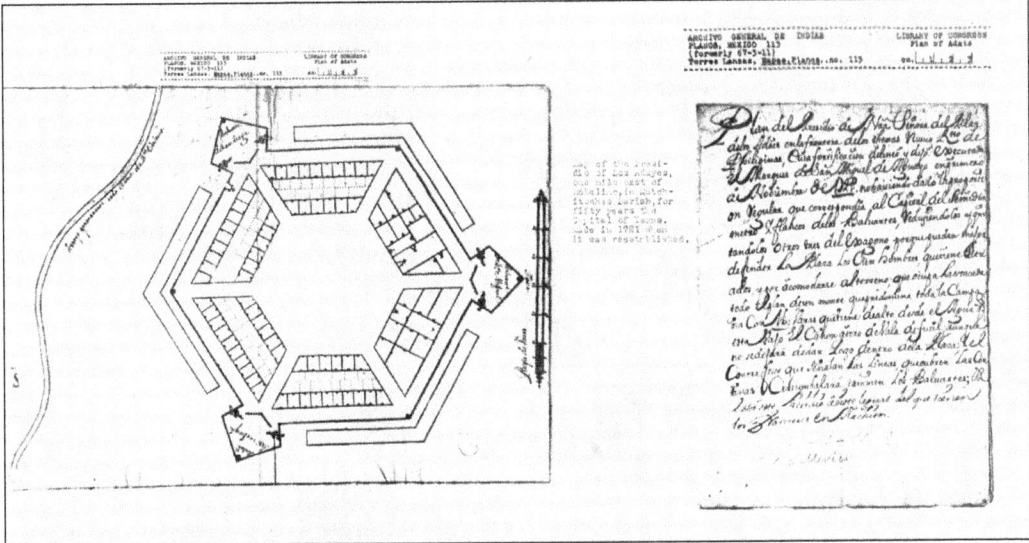

The Presidio at Los Adaes was part of the Colonial Spanish mission and was located nine miles southwest of Natchitoches. Los Adaes dates to the early 1700s when Fr. Francisco Hidelgo, a Franciscan missionary from New Spain, which is now Mexico, urged the Spanish governor to establish a post near east Texas. Even though Spain and France were often at war, the colonists at Los Adaes and Fort St. Jean Baptiste often traded goods so that each colony could survive. The Los Adaes archaeological site is now part of the Louisiana State Parks Commemorative Area. It is located one mile northeast of Robeline on Louisiana Highway 485.

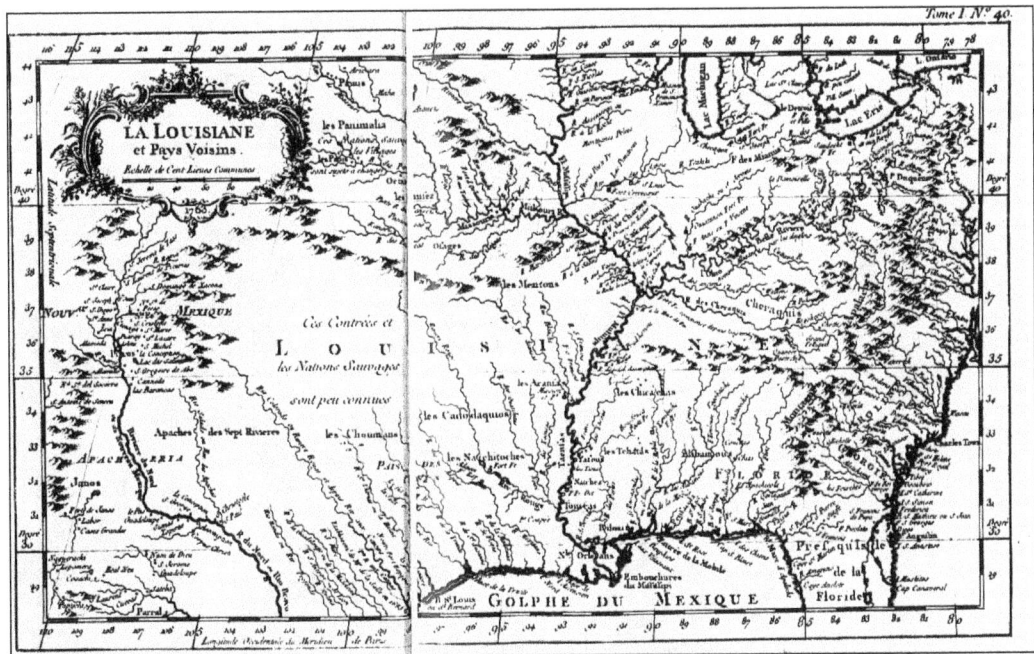

A French map shows the area that was purchased by the United States from France in 1803 and became known as The Louisiana Purchase. In 2003, Louisiana will celebrate the bicentennial of The Louisiana Purchase.

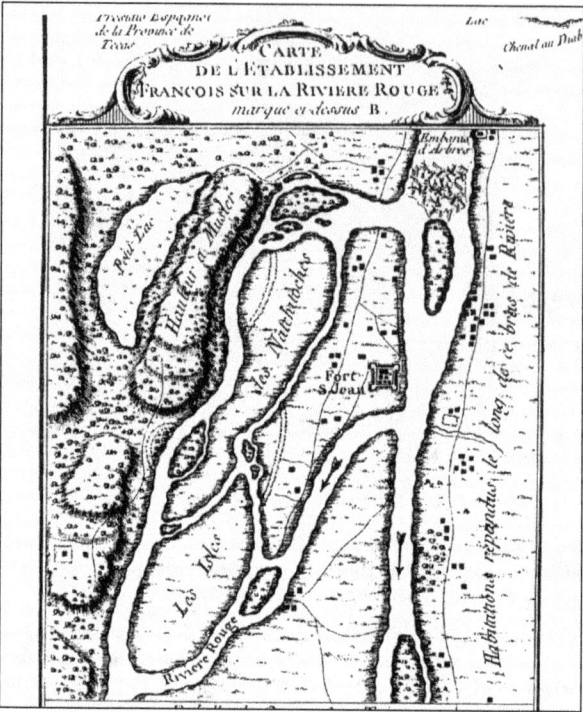

Natchitoches was occupied by the Natchitoches Indians. St. Denis cultivated significant ties to the numerous native groups, and it was through these ties that trade and Fort St. Jean Baptist flourished. Included in this map is the Fort St. Jean Baptiste, the Red River, and the Small Lake.

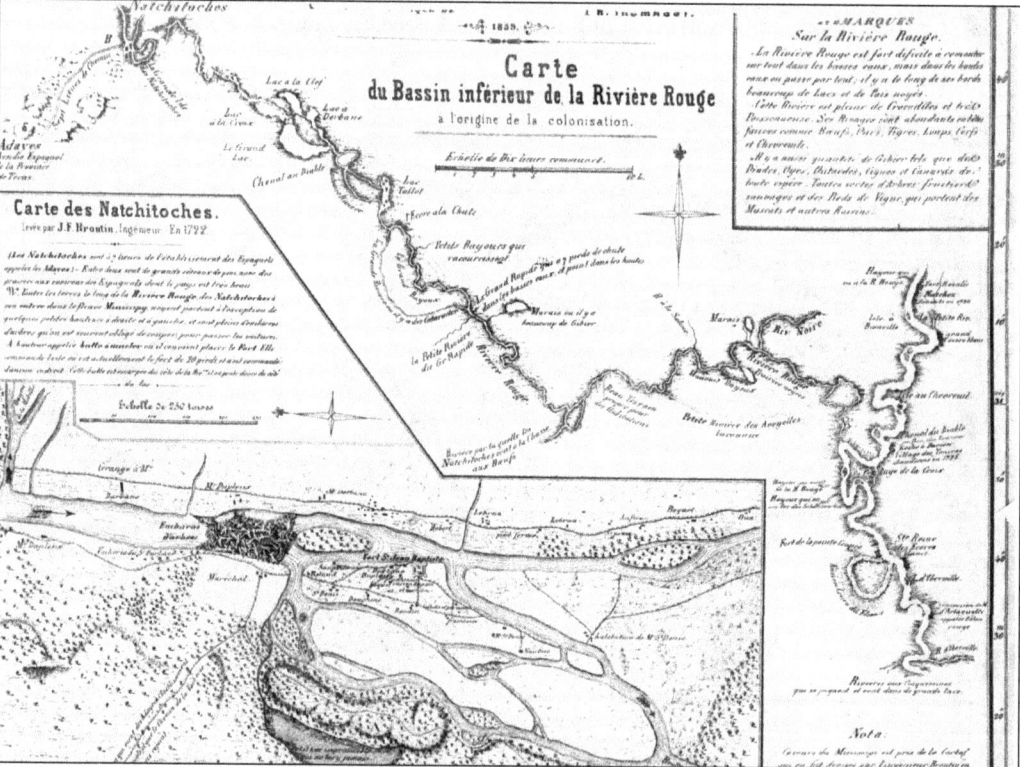

A colonial map depicts the intricate waterways in the town of Natchitoches and the site of Fort St. Jean Baptiste.

Two

HISTORIC HOUSES OF NATCHITOCHES

The St. Claire House was built c. 1870 by the St. Amant family and was located on a large lot at the corner of Williams and St. Claire Avenues. It was a raised plantation home of Greek Revival style. The house was demolished in the 1960s.

The Tauzin-Wells House is the oldest home in Natchitoches. It is constructed of hall timbers and bousillage, which is a mixture of hair, Spanish moss, and mud that is used as fill between hand-hewn wall timbers. The home was built by Gabriel Buard in 1776. The house was used for cotton seed storage until it was rescued and restored by Dr. and Mrs. W.T. Williams, who used the house as a home and doctor's office. The house was restored to its original appearance by Dr. Tom Wells and his wife, Carol.

Upon restoring the Tauzin-Wells house, Mrs. W.T. Williams planted the sunken gardens, which bloomed along Cane River.

Roselawn is considered to be the finest example of Queen Anne–style architecture in Louisiana. The house was given as a wedding gift from James Henry Williams Sr. to his second wife, Eliza Payne Williams, in 1903. It took three months to complete the construction of the house and it is painted in seven shades of green. The house received its name from the beautiful rose gardens planted by Eliza Payne Williams. It is located at 905 Williams Avenue.

J.H. and R.B. Williams, two of J.H. and Eliza Payne Williams's children, are seen riding ToGo ("Toe Go") at Roselawn c. 1914.

The Swett-Simmons House is an example of Queen Anne architecture. A U-shaped gallery extends the full width of the facade. In 1944, Scriven and Edwina Swett purchased the house. Scriven Swett was the clerk of court for Natchitoches Parish. The house is located at 621 Williams Avenue.

The DeBlieux-Sompayrac house was owned by Mr. and Mrs. Ambroise Sompayrac. It is a Creole-style, bousillage house, which was built in the 1800s and was originally raised off the ground. In 1971, Gene Smith moved the house from Red River near Clarance to its present location on Williams Avenue.

J. Ambroise Sompayrac was born in France in 1779. After he married Josephine Desiree Briant, they left France and traveled to Louisiana via the West Indies around 1800. They resided at Sompayrac plantation on the Red River at what is today Grand Ecore, Louisiana. The Sompayracs also owned a town house, which was located on Rue Washington near its intersection with Rue Pavie. The town house was torn down c. 1900.

Mrs. Josephine Desiree Briant Sompayrac was the daughter of Col. Francois Briant and Marie Elisabeth Mazard of Paris, France. She came with her husband to Natchitoches and they settled at Sompayrac Plantation at Grand Ecore.

17

The Tauzin Plantation House is a three-story, Creole-style structure that was built between 1830 and 1840 by Marcellin Tauzin, a Frenchman whose family arrived in Natchitoches in the late 1700s. The second and third stories are constructed of hand-hewn and pegged cypress timbers. The upstairs hallway is 40 feet long and features heart of pine floors. The house is located at 1950 Williams Avenue.

The original Lecomte Creole town house was located on Rue Front. It was demolished c. 1900 to make room for the new Lecomte Hotel, which was later named the Wemp Hotel and finally the Nakatosh Hotel.

The Nakatosh Hotel originally consisted of two stories. A third floor was later added. Several business were located in the hotel, including the St. Denis Restaurant, People's Bank, Milspaugh Drugstore, and Gongre's Barbershop. The Nakatosh Hotel remained in business until the 1960s.

The New Inn Hotel was the home of Jean Baptiste Prud'homme. Built c. 1795, it was located on the corner of Rue Front and Rue Touline and was later converted into the hotel. It was one of the most prominent Creole town houses in Natchitoches. This photograph shows the New Inn Hotel looking south.

The Kaffie-Moncla House is a multi-colored, Queen Anne–style house. It was the residence of the Kaffies, a prominent Jewish family in Natchitoches. The house was built c. 1890.

The Prud'homme Rouquier House was built by Francois Rouquier for his wife, Marie Louise Prud'homme, in the late 1700s or early 1800s. It is the largest bousillage house in Louisiana. Between 1834 and 1845, it was remodeled into the Greek Revival style that can be seen today. The house has recently been restored by the Natchitoches Service League from grants and monies received through the sale of its cookbook, *Cane River Cuisine*. The house is located at 436 Rue Jefferson.

Tante Huppe' ("Who-pay") was built c. 1851. It is an example of Greek Revival architecture and contains an attached slave quarters. The home has been associated with some of the oldest Creole families in Natchitoches, including the Lafon, Lecomte, Prud'homme, and Huppe' families. It is located at 424 Rue Jefferson.

The St. Amant-Tucker House was of Spanish design and contained an interior courtyard. It was located across the street from Tante Huppe' on Rue Jefferson. Dismantled in the 1950s for the construction of the new Natchitoches library, the house contained the oldest Spanish and French law libraries in Louisiana. The library was donated to the Louisiana State University law school and became the nucleus of the university's library.

The Metoyer town house was owned by the Creole planter Benjamin Metoyer and was built *c.* 1850. The Metoyer family sold the house to Joseph Henry, who sold the house to the Natchitoches Parish Police Jury in 1916. The policy jury converted the house into a parish hospital. The house is one of the finest examples of Creole town house–style architecture in Natchitoches and is located at 132 Rue Jefferson.

The Buard House was built *c.* 1840 and was located on the corner of Rue Jefferson and Rue Amulet. The Buard family was one of the oldest and most prominent European Creole families in Natchitoches. During the Union army's occupation of Natchitoches, two of the Buard girls who lived in the house were not allowed to open the house shutters or go outdoors.

Taken by Arthur Babb in 1927, these photographs show fire destroying the Buard house.

The Levy-East House was built by Italian architect Athaneze Trizzini as an office and home for Dr. Nichola Michel Friedelezy, a French Canadian, c. 1840. Dr. Friedelezy practiced medicine out of the house until it was discovered that his medical license was a forgery and he was forced to leave Natchitoches. In 1891, Leopold and Justine Dreyfus Levy purchased the house. It is located at 358 Rue Jefferson.

Maison Louisiane was built for Giovanni and Maria Theresa Delmonico Rusca in the 1880s. It is an example of Queen Anne–style architecture. The Ruscas raised nine children in the house. Giovanni Rusca opened a grocery store next to his house, which was located at 332 Rue Jefferson, the intersection of Rue Jefferson and Rue Poete.

The Taylor House was built by Louis Dupleix, a native of France, who came to Natchitoches in 1848. The house formerly stood directly on the street with the sidewalks passing under the columned portico. Louis Dupleix was owner of the "Natchitoches Union" prior to the Civil War. After the war, he was appointed by President Ulysses S. Grant as registrar of the U.S. Land Office.

Around 1910, the house was dismantled, the site was moved back, and it was rebuilt where it stands today. In the summer of 1988, the house was the location of the wedding scene in the movie *Steel Magnolias*.

The Lemee House was built by Joseph Soldini in 1837 and designed by his partner, Italian architect Athaneze Trizzini. Trizzini's family resided in the house until it was sold to the Union Bank of New Orleans for use as its Natchitoches branch. Alex Lemee was sent to manage the branch, but he decided to purchase the house as his residence. By 1940, the house was in total disrepair. Soon after, a group of architects came to Natchitoches with the "Historic House Survey" and one architect tried to purchase the house. The Association for the Preservation of Historic Natchitoches pressured the city fathers to purchase the home and donate it to their group for restoration. The association still operates the Lemee House as its headquarters.

The Soldini House, located at 240 Rue Jefferson, was designed by Italian architect Athaneze Trizzini for his partner, Joseph Soldini. A brick layer, Soldini purchased the lot from Mrs. Charles Greneaux and built the house. In 1858 he sold it to Chichester Chaplin Sr. The house was originally a one-and-a-half story Greek Revival house with a gallery across the front and back. In 1925, it was totally remodeled into the vernacular Italian Renaissance style seen today.

The Pierson House was originally built by a Professor Davis who taught at Louisiana Normal. However, Professor Davis died before he moved into the house. The house was purchased by J.H. Williams Sr. as a dowry house for his daughter, Ruth, who was married to Mr. Guthrie Henry Williams. Robert E. Lucky Jr. restored the house in 1972.

The Phillips House was built as a town house by an unknown Creole family c. 1830s. The house had a wrought iron gallery on three sides and was located at the intersection of Rue Jefferson and Rue Pine. It was demolished in the 1920s.

The Steamboat House was reportedly built by Captain Haynes out of two dismantled steamboats. The house is located at 200 Rue Jefferson.

The Nelken house was built for Samuel and Sarah Abrams Nelken in 1902. Samuel Nelken was born in Poland in 1847 and became a prominent merchant and land owner in Natchitoches. The Nelkens raised eight children in their home, located at 170 Rue Jefferson.

The Russell House was associated with the Pierson family. It was built in 1853 for Miss Gussie Pierson, who later married John Levy. The house was located on top of the hill at the corner of Rue Lafayette and Rue Second. The house was demolished in the 1960s.

The Dranguet House was built by Benjamin F. Dranguet *c.* 1835. An example of Greek Revival architecture and constructed of bricks, the house is located at 146 Rue Jefferson.

The House of the Brides was built c. 1790 and was one of Natchitoches's oldest homes. The only thing that remains from the house today is a large circular medallion in bas-relief (deep cut moldings). The medallion is located in the Louisiana State Museum in Natchitoches. The house was located on the corner of Rue Second and Rue Sibley and was demolished in the early 1960s.

The Chaplin House was built for Thomas P. Chaplin and his wife, Lise Breazeale Chaplin, in 1892. The house an example of Victorian architecture and was constructed almost entirely by a man named Zeno, who performed the work without the benefit of architectural drawings or plans. The house is located at 434 Rue Second.

The Old Breazeale House was a Victorian-style home that was built c. 1880–1890 on the corner of Rue Second and Rue Touline. It was demolished in the 1970s.

The Judge Porter House was built in 1912 for Thomas and Wilhelmina Porter. It is located at the corner of Rue Second and Rue Poete. Another building, the Blunt Lodge Hall, was located on the property and many of its materials were used in the construction of the Judge Porter House. It took three months to construct the house at a cost of $1,500.

The Judge Porter House is two stories, has 33 windows, and 31,000 square feet. Five fireplaces were constructed within the house and several live oaks, which were planted by Judge Porter in 1912, can be found on the property today. The Judge Porter house is seen covered in snow.

Judge Thomas Fitzgerald Porter was born in 1854. He graduated from Thatcher's Institute in Shreveport and then spent two years in the Western United States before returning to Louisiana and settling in Natchitoches. Porter later married Wilhelmina Henrietta Dunckleman in 1880 and five children were born of the marriage. Judge Porter was a farmer, was elected to the Natchitoches Parish Policy Jury, and was also elected Natchitoches Parish Assessor. It was in this position that he received the honorary title of "judge." Judge Porter died in his home in 1928.

Wilhelmina Dunckleman Porter was born in Natchitoches in 1855 and was of German descent. Her parents were German immigrants who settled in Natchitoches. She married Thomas Fitzgerald Porter in 1880, and the two of them were instrumental in the construction of the First United Methodist Church and were the first couple to be married in the church. Mrs. Porter rented her home to boarders. Male boarders were not allowed to bathe inside the Porter home and instead had to bathe in Bayou Amulet, which runs behind the house. Boarders were required to share rooms, with at least two beds per room, and the rent was $2 per week.

The St. Denis Oak is a red oak that is more than 275 years old. A legend exists that the only daughter of Zomach, the chief of the Natchitoches Indians, jumped off a bluff and died when she discovered that the Spanish soldier she loved had returned to Spain. St. Denis marked her grave by planting a red oak in her memory.

The American Cemetery is the oldest cemetery in the Louisiana Purchase. It is believed that the second Fort St. Jean Baptiste was erected on what is now the grounds of the American Cemetery. Buried within its grounds are the colonists' first descendants, along with descendants of European participants of every major war involving American troops. St. Denis is also believed to be have been buried in the cemetery upon his death in 1744.

This picture, taken by Arthur Babb in 1927, is of the grave of Dame Marie Anne D'Artigaux, who died in 1797. This is the oldest known grave in the American Cemetery.

The Boozman House is a Creole cottage that was built c. 1900. The house was owned by State Representative Curtis Boozman. It is presently named the American Inn and is located at 212 Rue Second.

The Magnolias is one of the most significant Greek Revival homes in Natchitoches and was built c. 1805. The house has had nine names, including Lauve, Pavie, Tauzin, Lecomte, St. Amant, Gentry, Walmsley, and Carroll. Legend has it that Gen. James Wilkerson was living in this house when he received a coded message from Aaron Burr, dated July 29, 1806. Shortly thereafter, General Wilkerson sent a letter to President Thomas Jefferson, informing him of the Burr Conspiracy. However, some historians believe that General Wilkerson resided in another house near the Magnolias that is now demolished. The Magnolias is located at 902 Rue Washington.

The Breazeale House was built by Phanor Breazeale in 1910. It is an example of a Colonial Revival residence. Phanor Breazeale was elected to the United States Senate and was responsible for passing legislation that allowed a dam to be constructed across the lower portion of Cane River. The dam kept the waters of the Red River from backing up into Natchitoches. This is why the river that runs through downtown Natchitoches is called Cane River Lake. The house is located at 926 Rue Washington.

The Chamard-Dunahoe house is French-Colonial in style and dates to c. 1760. The first recorded transfer of ownership of the house was in 1768 from Commandant Caesar Borme of Fort St. Jean Baptiste to Andre Chamard, a French descendant of the Bourbon family who was knighted by Louis XIV of France. It is believed that the house was built by soldiers, slaves, and Native Americans. Future residents of the house were Col. William H. Jack, who purchased the house in 1873 for $5,000. Colonel Jack was a prominent judge in north Louisiana and the grandfather of famous short story writer, Ada Jack Carver. Colonel Jack owned numerous exotic birds, including peacocks, pheasants, and eagles, which lived in his backyard. The house is located at 120 Rue Amulet.

The Roque House was built by a freed black slave named "Yves," but called "Pacale," in 1797. The house took six years to build and Pacale and his family resided in it until 1816. The house was purchased by Charles Nerespere Roque, a free person of color, who was a planter and slave owner. When his son, Aubin Roque, married Marie Philomene Augustin Metoyer, the daughter of Augustin Metoyer, the newlyweds moved into the house. In 1967, under the direction of Robert, "Bobby" DeBlieux, the Roque House was moved from its original location, between Bermuda and Isle Brevelle, by Museum Contents, Inc., a local historical preservation group, to its present site along the banks of Cane River in downtown Natchitoches. The house is now the office of the Cane River Heritage Area Commission.

The Laureate House is a brick antebellum home that was built for Antonio Balzaretti c. 1840. The legal title for the lot, upon which the Laureate House stands, was given to Louis Lambre by the Spanish in 1791. The house was restored by the late Ruby Smitha Dunckleman, who was head of the economics department at Northwestern. The house is located at 225 Rue Poete.

The Rusca house was built for Joseph Delmonico and Pearl Kile Rusca in 1920. The house is a bungalow style and contains heart of pine floors and a Creole-style fireplace mantel, which suggests it was moved to the house from an antebellum home. Joseph Delmonico Rusca was a prominent attorney and resided in the house until his death in the late 1960s. The house is located at 124 Rue Poete.

The Queen Anne is a Victorian-style home that was built in 1905 by Charles J. and Annie Green. Charles J. Green was a Civil War veteran who lived in the house until his death in 1934. Annie Green also remained in the house until her death. The house remained in the Green family until the Greens' oldest daughter, Ms. Jessie Green, died in 1965. In this photograph, C.J. Green Sr. is shown with his son, Rob Green, daughter, Annie Green, and dog, Rex, at the Queen Anne c. 1907. The home is located at 125 Rue Pine.

The Green family is pictured at the Queen Anne c. 1929.

Green Gables, which is also known as the Elizabeth Bryant Sutton House, is located at 201 Rue Pine and is a Queen Anne, Victorian-style house. It was built at the turn of the century by Estelle Ducournau Plauche and given as a wedding gift to her niece, whose name is unknown. Estelle Plauche's niece married a doctor from New York, and they resided in the house for two years before they returned to New York. It is unknown who resided in the house from the early 1900s until the 1930s, when it was purchased by Elizabeth Bryant Sutton. Ms. Sutton resided in the house until 1992, when it was purchased by Linda Lou Ropp. At that time, Ms. Sutton was 104 years old. The house was restored by Linda Lou Ropp.

The Breda Plantation House was located in what is now Lakeland Subdivision. It was built by Jean Philippe Breda and his wife, Marie Drangnet, c. 1840. The house was demolished c. 1900.

42

Three

CANE RIVER PLANTATIONS

Oak Lawn plantation was built by Achille Prud'homme between 1830 and 1840 by slave labor using materials that were found on the plantation. Achille Prud'homme died in 1864 and his widow saved the house from passing Union troops by dressing a child in a scarlet cloak, which was the symbol of scarlet fever. She positioned the child on the gallery as a warning. The Prud'homme family lost the house to carpetbaggers after the Civil War, but bought it back in 1915.

Oak Lawn is three stories tall and features a steep hip roof with 14 interior chimneys and a large gallery that surrounds three sides. The house contains 20 feet of folding French doors with hand-blown glass panes. Oak Lawn is now owned by Robert Harling, author of the play and movie *Steel Magnolias*. Robert Harling has restored the house to its original beauty.

Beau Fort Plantation was built by Louis Barthalamew Rachal in 1790 and sold at his succession. It was purchased by Emmanuel Prud'homme of Oakland Plantation and given to his son, L. Narcisse Prud'homme. The house is made of bousillage and is Creole in style.

In 1948, Mr. and Mrs. Vernon Cloutier restored Beau Fort. Included with the house was a stranger's room, which had a separate entrance and was set aside solely for the use of travelers. Beau Fort is presently owned by Mr. and Mrs. Jack O. Brittain Sr.

The Keator House was located about one-half of a mile north of Oakland Plantation on Cane River. The house was of Victorian style and was built c. 1900. It was originally owned by Antoine Prud'homme, brother of Emanuel Prud'homme of Oakland Plantation.

Numa Lambre owned Lambre Plantation, which was located between Beau Fort and Oak Lawn. Mr. Lambre was a very wealthy European Creole. Lambre Plantation was built c. 1850 and is no longer in existence.

Cherokee Plantation was purchased by Emile Sompayrac from his father-in-law, Narcisse Prud'homme, in 1839. A house located on the site was restored by Emile and Clairesse Sompayrac. After Emile's death in 1891, the house was sold several times and eventually purchased by Robert Calvert Murphy. Murphy's granddaughter, Mrs. Theodosia Nolan, and her husband restored Cherokee. The savannah at the rear of the house was the scene of the famous Bossier-Gaiennie duel, at which Gen. Francois Gaiennie of Cloutierville was killed by Gen. Pierre Evariste Bossier.

Oakland Plantation was built in 1821 by Emmanuel Prud'homme. The plantation complex contains 14 buildings of bousillage construction. The house contains its original furnishings, paintings, and family library. A blacksmith slave at Oakland named Soloman made the first wrought-iron well drilling equipment. The house was saved during the Civil War by the plantation's slaves, who begged the Union army not to burn the house.

Emmanuel Prud'homme planted the first cotton in Louisiana along with indigo and tobacco; he also served in the first session of the Louisiana legislature. Prud'homme suffered from severe bouts of pain, thought to be arthritis, and was informed by the Natchitoches Indians of a place that contained healing waters. In 1807, he traveled with the Indians to what is now Hot Springs, Arkansas. He was one of the first white settlers to visit this area and he built a home there.

The Prud'homme family is seen on vacation in Hot Springs, Arkansas.

Lestan Prud'homme Jr. was born and lived at Oakland Plantation. He was wounded in the leg during the Civil War at the siege of Vicksburg. At the end of the war, he returned to Natchitoches, where he lived the rest of his life at Willow Plantation on Red River. His diary is featured in Lyle Saxton's book, *Old Louisiana*.

The Jean Baptiste Metoyer House was a raised Creole plantation house, which was built by Jean Baptiste Metoyer, *c.* 1830. The house burned in the 1960s.

Cammie Henry was born at Scatterly Plantation in Ascension Parish in 1871. She married John Hampton Henry and they moved to Melrose Plantation, which had formerly been called Yucca Plantation and had been owned by the descendants of Marie Thereze Coincoin. Melrose had been decimated by years of neglect, but through long hours of perseverance, Cammie Henry restored the architecture, buildings, and gardens.

Melrose Plantation was originally named Yucca Plantation and was owned by Louis Metoyer, the son of Thomas Pierre Metoyer, a wealthy French Creole planter, and Marie Thereze Coincoin, a slave born in 1742 and owned by St. Denis, the founder of Natchitoches. The couple had 10 children, who were all freed. The Big House at Melrose was built in 1833 by Louis Metoyer, the son of Thomas Metoyer and Marie Thereze Coincoin. The Big House was restored by Cammie Henry during her years at Melrose.

Nicolas Augustin Metoyer, the eldest son of Claude Thomas Pierre Metoyer and Marie Thereze Coincoin, was born on August 1, 1768. Three weeks after receiving his freedom from his father, he married Marie Agnes Poissot in 1792. Nine children were born of this marriage. In 1795 he founded the Isle Brevelle colony. His plantation, Yucca, was very successful.

This portrait of Mrs. Augustin Metoyer is believed to have been painted by Jules Lion of New Orleans in the 1840s.

Marie Thereze Carmelite Anty Metoyer was the daughter of Marie Suzanne Metoyer and granddaughter of Marie Thereze Coincoin and Claude Thomas Pierre Metoyer. She was the twin sister of Nicholas Augustin Metoyer. This portrait was also believed to have been painted by Jules Lion of New Orleans in the 1840s.

53

The Badin-Roque House is a unique structure of Poteau Terre ("posts in the ground") construction. This was a common construction method prior to 1820. The house was built in the early 1800s with a single central chimney and dirt floors. It is the last house in Louisiana of this type of construction and only four remain in the United States.

In the early 1820s, Augustin Metoyer and his brother Louis Metoyer donated the land and supplied the labor for the construction of St. Augustine Catholic Church. The original church was erected in 1829 and is no longer present. The current church was built c. 1880 and mass is still performed there every day.

Cammie Henry invited writers, poets, and painters to use Melrose as a place to produce their work. One of the most famous short story writers of the 1920s, Ada Jack Carver wrote at Melrose. Her short story, "Redbone," which is set in Isle Brevelle, was a critical success and received the O. Henry Memorial Award and the Harper Magazine's Prize in 1925.

Lyle Saxon was a writer in residence at Melrose for several years. He wrote several books at Melrose, including *Lafitte the Pirate*, *Father Mississippi*, and *Fabulous New Orleans*. Saxon's only novel, *Children of Strangers*, is set at Melrose. It is said that Cammie Henry often locked Lyle Saxon in the Yucca House to force him to complete *Children of Strangers*.

Yucca House was the original main house at Melrose and was built in 1776 by Marie Thereze Coincoin. Many noted artists, writers, and poets resided in Yucca during their stay at Melrose. Francois Mignon is seen standing in the entrance to the Yucca House.

The African House was built in the late 1700s at Melrose and is the only structure of Congo architecture in North America. The house was used as a storehouse and jail for rebellious slaves.

Uncle Israel was a worker at Melrose who lived in the Yucca House for many years. After years of praying, Uncle Israel revealed that the Lord had appeared to him and had granted him the ability to read, if he only read the Bible. Uncle Israel became the preacher at Primitive Rock Church, which was located across Cane River form Melrose. Over the years, when Uncle Israel became too feeble to walk to church, Cammie Henry had a buggy take him to his church services. Uncle Israel suffered from palsy in the last years of his life. Each night, Cammie Henry would take supper to Uncle Israel and feed him with her finest silver utensils. Upon Uncle Israel's death, Cammie Henry prepared him for his coffin and saw that a proper burial was given for him.

Clementine Hunter moved to Melrose Plantation at the age of five or six. She picked cotton and pecans at the plantation until the 1920s, when she became a maid and cook at the Big House. In 1940, Clementine Hunter started painting. She gave her first painting to Francois Mignon.

Clementine Hunter is pictured outside of her art exhibit. For a quarter, people could view her artwork. Her earlier paintings, which now sell for thousands of dollars, could be purchased for a few dollars.

"Plantation Harvest" was painted in 1979. Clementine Hunter painted life at Melrose Plantation. This painting includes the Big House and the African House. Clementine painted mostly at night after working a full day at the Big House.

"Saturday Night at the Honky Tonk" was painted in 1963. Clementine Hunter painted on anything she or Francois Mignon could find, including cardboard boxes, the inside of soap cartons, brown paper bags, pieces of wood, and window shades. At first, her primary source of paint was discarded tubes from various artists who had worked at Melrose.

"Funeral" was painted in 1950. In 1955, Clementine Hunter became the first black artist to have her own show at The Delgado Museum, which is now the New Orleans Museum of Art. Also in 1955, at the age of 68, she pained the top floor of the African House during a three-month period. The painting consisted of nine large panels and several small connecting panels, which encircled the room and depicted the story of the Cane River Country.

Over the years, Clementine Hunter became a legendary folk artist. In 1976, her work was included in the United Nations UNICEF calendar. Her artwork has been featured by several universities and at major art exhibitions in New York, California, and Washington, D.C. This picture was taken of Clementine by Curtis Guillet.

60

Ambrose Lecomte II started work on Magnolia Plantation's Big House in 1830, when he was 23 years old. The house was burned by the Union army during the Civil War but was rebuilt by Matthew Hertzog in 1889, using the same massive brick pillars, walls, and foundations of the original home. The house is of Greek Revival style. Magnolia has the only row of brick slave quarters still standing in Louisiana. It also has preserved a cotton gin containing a historic cypress mule-drawn cotton press, a Creole overseer's house, a general store, a blacksmith shop, and the pigeonnierre, a large cage where pigeons and other birds are raised.

Ambrose Lecomte was born in Natchitoches in 1807. In 1827, he married Marie Julie Buard of Natchitoches. He was a wealthy planter and turfman and was the owner of the famous race horses Lecomte and Flying Dutchman. This portrait was painted by Louis Antoine Collas when Ambrose Lecomte was 21 years old.

Madame Ambrose Lecomte was born in Natchitoches in 1809. She was the daughter of Jean Louis Buard and Eulalie Emilie Bossier. Her family was one of the oldest European Creole families in Natchitoches. This portrait was painted by Louis Antoine Collas in 1928 when Madame Ambrose Lecomte was 19 years old.

The Kate Chopin House is also known as the Bayou Folk Museum and is located in Cloutierville, on Highway 1, 12 miles south of Natchitoches. The house was built by Alexis Cloutier in the mid-1800s. Oscar and Kate Chopin moved to Cloutierville and purchased the house in 1879, after Oscar Chopin's business had failed in New Orleans. It was during Kate Chopin's years in Cloutierville that she was inspired to write her famous stories of plantation life on lower Cane River. Her collection of short stories, called *Bayou Folks*, was published in 1894. Her most famous novel, *The Awakening*, was published in 1899.

Kate O'Flaherty Chopin was born in St. Louis in 1851. At the age of 19, she married Oscar Chopin, a French-Creole from Louisiana. They resided in New Orleans until 1879 when they moved to Cloutierville. Four years later, Oscar Chopin died of swamp fever. At the time of Oscar Chopin's death, Kate Chopin was 31 and had six children under the age of 12. She remained in Cloutierville and ran the Chopin's plantation and store for more than a year before she returned to St. Louis. Over the next several years, Kate Chopin started to write poetry. In 1889, her first poem was published. Her subsequent works were published in *Vogue*, *Atlantic Monthly*, and *Harper's Young People*. In 1899, at the age of 48, she published *The Awakening*, which was very controversial and banned by numerous libraries. In 1904, Kate Chopin died of a brain hemorrhage. It was not until decades later that *The Awakening* received literary acceptance.

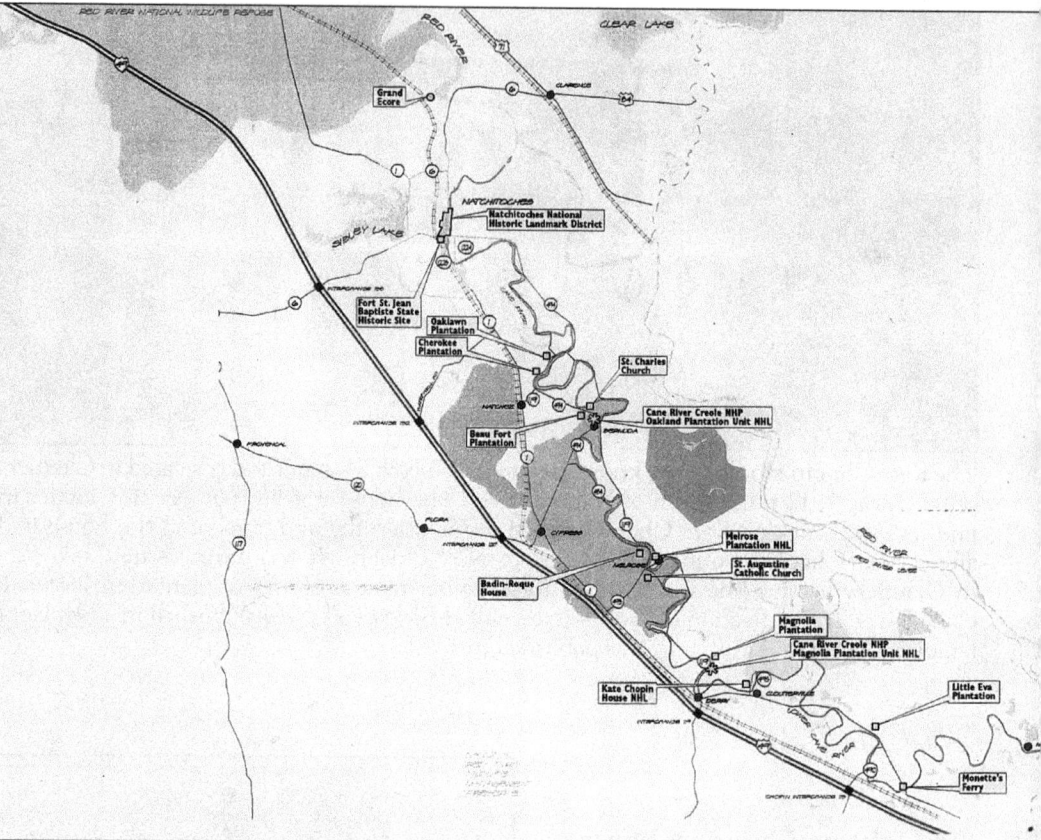

The Cane River National Heritage Area is located primarily in Natchitoches Parish and includes five National Historic sites, three State Historic Areas, the Cane River Creole National Historic Park, and many historic plantations, homes, and churches. This area includes a mixture of cultures that have lived in Natchitoches Parish for the past 300 years, including Europeans, free and enslaved African Americans, Native Americans, and Creoles of French, African, Spanish, and American Indian descent. The purpose of the Heritage Area is to preserve the culture, buildings, and customs of this unique and historic area.

Four

PLANTATIONS OF
NATCHITOCHES PARISH

The Marco Plantation House was built by Nicola Gratia in the 1820s or 1830s. The house was sold in 1860 to Marco Givanovich and comprised 5,740 acres, 50 slaves, a large number of mules, and farming implements. The house was located on the old Red River, which was later Cane River, near the outlet to Colfax. The house was dismantled in the early 1900s and its great, winding staircase was salvaged by Cammie Henry and brought to Melrose. Mrs. Cammie built a small house kitchen around it, which was later destroyed by a fire in the 1950s.

Hidden Hill Plantation is located several miles south of Melrose. It is considered by some historians to have been the inspiration for the book, *Uncle Tom's Cabin*. Renowned folk artist Clementine Hunter was born at Hidden Hill Plantation in either late December 1886 or early January 1887.

The Roubieu-Carol Jones House is a two-story, white Creole house with a green roof. Francois Roubieu, a wealthy European Creole, built this house in 1814–1815.

Willow Plantation was built by Alexander Louis DeBlieux *c.* 1825. Willow was used by the Union army as a hospital after the Battle of Mansfield and Pleasant Hill. When the Union army retreated from the hospital, it removed all of the furnishings and even some of the glass out of the windows. Alexander Louis DeBlieux received restitution from the federal government after the Civil War due to his friendship with President Ulysses S. Grant. This photograph shows the rear view of the Willow Plantation House.

St. Maurice Plantation was built in 1826 by Dennis Fort. The house was of Greek Revival architecture and was located in St. Maurice, in rural Natchitoches Parish. The house was owned by the William Prothro family from 1846 until 1856 and by Dr. David H. Boullt in 1856. The El Camino Real, which means "The Kings Highway," ran in front of the house. The house was destroyed by a fire in the 1970s.

The Cook House is a Greek Revival house that was built in the 1850s on the Ellzey Plantation near Robeline. In the 1880s, upon the completion of the Texas & Pacific railroad, J.E. Keegan purchased the house from the Ellzey estate. The house was disassembled and then moved to its present location in Robeline. The house was used as a hotel for railroad passengers.

Five

CHURCHES, SCHOOLS, BUILDINGS, AND LAGNIAPPE

The first fire engine in Natchitoches was bought in 1891 for the Perseverance Fire Company Number One. It was built by the Silsby Manufacturing Company of Seneca Falls, New York, and cost $3,500. The fire engine was christened the *Julie C.* in honor of Miss Julia Caspari, who was the daughter of Captain Caspari and was considered the most beautiful young lady of Natchitoches. The fire engine was permanently named *Rough and Ready*.

CATHEDRAL, NATCHITOCHES, LA.

Immaculate Conception Church is the sixth Catholic church built in Natchitoches. It was begun in 1856, but it took almost 30 years before it was completed. Bishop Martin and Vicar-General P.F. Dicharry are buried in the church. The original crystal chandeliers and the baptismal font remain. The first Mass west of the Mississippi was said here.

The Catholic Rectory was the first prefabricated building in Louisiana. It was built in New Orleans and shipped to Natchitoches in 1885. It exhibits architectural features of the Italian and Second Empire styles. Baptismal records dating back to 1723 are housed here. Also located on the grounds of the Catholic Rectory is the Bishop Martin Museum.

Fr. Anthony Piegay is pictured here with altar boys in 1916. Fr. Piegay was born in 1862 and was ordained a priest in 1887. He became Vicar General in 1905. He was an assistant and pastor of Immaculate Conception Church for 52 years.

This is the third Catholic Cemetery; the first was located in Fort St. Jean Baptiste and the second was located on Rue Church, directly behind a small chapel that faced Rue Front. In the 1850s, the cemetery was moved to its present site, which is at the foot of Rue Church and Rue Fourth.

The first permanent Trinity Episcopal Church was built in 1843 and located at the corner of Rue Front and Rue Trudeau. The present church was built in 1857 and the first service was held on Ash Wednesday 1858. Funds to build the church were donated by Gen. J. Watts de Peyster of New York, in memory of his daughter, Marie La de Peyster, who died in 1857. The silver communion vessels given by de Peyster are still used today.

SECOND STREET, NATCHITOCHES, LA.

The architect of the Trinity Episcopal Church was Frank Willis of New York. The church has distinctive Romanesque features and was the first non-Catholic church in Natchitoches. It is the third-oldest Episcopal church in Louisiana. The parish house and classroom building were added in 1962.

The First Baptist Church congregation was organized in 1879 and a church was built on the corner of Rue Second and Rue Church. The First Baptist Church is now located on Rue Second and Rue Touline and was constructed in 1929.

The First Presbyterian Church in Natchitoches was built in 1912 and was located on the corner of Rue Touline and Rue Second, where the new Natchitoches library is currently located. In 1920, lightning struck the church and it burned. The church was rebuilt in 1921 and was demolished in the 1960s.

The original First United Methodist Church was built in 1880 on the corner of Rue Second and Rue Lafayette, and it was sold in 1913. The congregation built the church pictured here in 1913, and it was dismantled in 1953. The third church burned in 1954.

The present First United Methodist Church was built in the same location and has recently been refurbished. The church is located at 411 Rue Second.

The first Natchitoches Parish Courthouse was built in 1827 and demolished in 1888, when the police jury determined that the slate roof could not be stopped from leaking. It was located on the corner of Rue Church and Rue Second.

Construction on the second Natchitoches Parish Courthouse began in 1896. It is an example of Romanesque Revival architecture and now houses the State Museum.

The first St. Mary's Academy, was established by the Sisters of Divine Providence in 1888. It was located on a hill overlooking Rue Touline. St. Mary's Academy was later expanded to two buildings located on the same hill.

The old and new St. Mary's Academy buildings are pictured here. The house on the left dates to 1846 and was occupied by the Sacred Heart Order, who resided there until 1856. The buildings were then used for St. Joseph College, which had been established by Bishop Martin. The college was subsequently removed and the house again was occupied as a convent by the Sisters of Mercy in 1870. The Sisters of Mercy left in 1878 and the buildings remained vacant until St. Mary's Academy was established in 1888 by five Sisters of Divine Providence, who arrived from San Antonio. St. Mary's School recently celebrated its 114th year of existence. The buildings shown in this picture no longer exist.

The old Natchitoches High School was located at Rue Third and Rue St. Denis. In the 1940s, the students moved to another school. The Catholic diocese bought the old building and transferred St. Mary's High School there. The second and third floors were made into a gymnasium. This building remained St. Mary's High School until *c.* 1967, when it was razed.

The Model School is pictured *c.* 1907 on the campus of Louisiana Normal. It included 8 grades and a high school along with 10 rooms with 35 pupils to each room. For two half-hour periods each day the lessons were given by the senior education majors under the watchful eye of their college professors.

The Natchitoches Grammar School is shown *c.* 1894. The school was run by Prof. and Mrs. Leon Greneaux. Professor Greneaux was a graduate of St. Louis University while Mrs. M. Greneaux was a graduate of St. Michael's Convent and Louisiana Normal.

A *c.* 1915 class picture shows students in front of the Natchitoches Grammar School. The number of students exceeded 100 and the school consisted of grade, middle, and high schools.

Due to the location of Cane River, many children traveled to school in Natchitoches by using the school boat *Pearl*.

The Cunningham Law Office was the law office of William S. Toumy II. The porch of the law office features Doric columns and a turned baluster railing. The house also contains rare twin central chimneys. The law office is the home of the Natchitoches Historic Foundation and is located at 550 Rue Second.

The old Natchitoches Parish jail was located on Rue Church, behind the second Natchitoches Parish Courthouse. This photograph shows the jail being built.

This was the first bank in Natchitoches, and today it is the Pioneer Pub. This building is located at 812 Rue Washington.

The lighting of the first gas pipes in Natchitoches at Breazeale's Fire Insurance Office on Rue St. Denis is seen *c*. 1926.

Above is Live Oak Corner in 1911. Next to the live oak was the Live Oak Hotel, which was located at the corner of Rue Second and Rue St. Denis. The Live Oak Hotel burned *c*. 1933.

This photograph shows Rue Second *c.* 1915. At this time, Rue Second was a dirt street. Trinity Episcopal Church, the second Nacthitoches Parish Courthouse, and Immaculate Conception Church can be seen in this photograph.

St. Denis Hotel, located on Rue St. Denis behind the Live Oak Hotel, is pictured here after a snowfall.

The Artist Colony was located on Rue Washington on Cane River approximately 200 yards north of Rue Texas. The Newcomb College School of Art in New Orleans used the art colony during the summers for class instruction by the famous artist Ellsworth Woodward.

The Uncle Jack statue, which is also known as the "Good Darkie" statue, was located at the northern end of Rue Front. The statue was eight feet high and was given to the city of Natchitoches by Mr. Joe Bryan. Mr. Bryan dedicated the statute in recognition of the black people of the antebellum South, whom he loved while growing up in Natchitoches Parish. The statue remained on Rue Front from 1927 until 1968, and it is now housed at the Louisiana State University Rural Life Museum in Baton Rouge.

An aerial view highlights downtown Natchitoches and Cane River. The Church Street Bridge, the Nakatosh Hotel, and the Immaculate Conception Church can be seen in this photograph.

This photograph of Natchitoches was taken from a water tower in July 1911. The Natchitoches Post office can be seen on the left and the Natchitoches Parish Jail can be seen on the right.

Six

DOWNTOWN
DEVELOPMENT

Rue Front is pictured at night during the 1950s. Some of the businesses included in this photograph, starting from the left, are P. & C. Rexall Drug Store, Nichol's Dry Goods, the People's Hardware Store, and Morgan & Lindsey.

Prior to the damming of Cane River, the water level on the river fluctuated greatly. At times the water level would drop low enough for people to cross it using a plank walk like the one shown here, c. 1914.

Farmers drive an ox team across the Cane River during the river's low water level, c. 1910.

The Youngstown Bridge Company started construction on the iron drawbridge that spanned Cane River in September 1893.

The construction was overseen by the Natchitoches Cane River Bridge Company, a corporation that was organized in 1890 to build the bridge.

The bridge was owned jointly by the City and Parish of Natchitoches. This photograph shows the Church Street Bridge, looking west.

The bridge was completed in February 1894. This photograph shows the first crossing of what became known as the Church Street Bridge.

CANE RIVER BRIDGE, NATCHITOCHES, LA.

The bridge was 16 feet wide and 480 feet long, and it cost $15,500.

The Church Street Bridge is pictured after a snowfall. Cane River is frozen and Natchitoches residents were able to cross it on foot. In the background is the Nakatosh Hotel.

Rue Front started to develop slowly, as can be seen from this photograph showing Rue Front at Rue Touline looking north. Rue Front is a dirt road.

Front Street, a part of Jefferson Highway.   Natchitoches, La.

This image shows Rue Front at the Nakatosh Hotel c. 1920s. Some of the business depicted in this photograph are McClung Drug, Antoon's Barbershop, Lewis's, DeBlieux's, West Bros. Department Store, and Devargas Jewelers.

This photograph shows Rue Front looking south. Some of the businesses, starting from the right, are Kaffie-Frederick Hardware Store, Reese's Variety Store, Todd's Department Store, Keegan's, Hughes, American Department Store, Levy Drug Co., and Kirkland Optometry.

Rue Front Street was bricked in the 1920s and it was expanded in the 1930s through the Works Progress Administration. During Earl Long's tenure as governor in the 1960s, the State Department of Highways wanted to remove the bricks and pave Rue Front. Numerous women in town literally laid down on the Rue Front in front of the highway department's bulldozers. When the highway department officials notified Governor Long, he asked how many women were involved. He was told over 100. Governor Long is reported to have said, "Turn the bulldozers around and let's go home."

Rue Front still contains the bricks that were placed there in the 1920s and 1930s. The bricks will soon be taken up, repaired, and returned to Rue Front.

This auction occurred during trade days on the banks of the Cane River

The citizens of Natchitoches enjoy a trade day's parade on Rue Front outside the Nakatosh Hotel and across Rue Church. During the day's parade, citizens would sell a variety of goods on Rue Front and along the banks of Cane River.

The citizens of Natchitoches enjoy an event occurring on the banks of Cane River while sitting on the hill overlooking the river.

Natchitoches has a long standing tradition of providing entertainment on Rue Front and along the banks of Cane River. The Natchitoches Brass Band was one of the first groups to start this tradition.

Natchitoches is best known as the City of Lights and for its annual Christmas festival, which occurs on the first Saturday in December. The Christmas festival was started in 1926 when Max Burgdof, the city's chief electrician, approached several local businesses, which put up money to purchase lights that were strung on Rue Front. Over the years, the lights were extended from Rue Front to encompass the entire downtown area. In addition, Max Burgdof and later Charles Solomon, the successor chief electrician, along with Charlie Maggio, built dozens of Christmas set pieces, which are still displayed today along the banks of Cane River.

The Christmas Festival started when small groups of people gathered downtown and watched the Christmas lights being turned on. Over time, the Natchitoches Chamber of Commerce organized an annual event, which occurs the first Saturday in December and includes a parade and fireworks. Today, the event attracts more than 100,000 spectators.

It is a tradition during the Natchitoches Christmas Festival parade that Santa Claus rides on the last float.

The City of Natchitoches has expanded the firework shows from the first Saturday in December to every Saturday in December and New Year's Eve.

A group of tourists enjoy a relaxing cruise down Cane River on a tour boat in the mid-1990s.

Seven

COMMERCE IN
NATCHITOCHES

Most goods transported to Natchitoches were taken by steamboat up the Red River to Cane River and then to downtown Natchitoches. Every farm had a landing. Shown are goods being removed from the *W.T. Scovell* on the banks of Cane River near Rue Front.

River Boat on Cane before above dam

The *W.T. Scovell* is pictured on the banks of Cane River near Rue Front in 1908.

The steamer *W.T. Scovell* is docked at Twenty-four Mile Landing, Cohen Plantation. Frank Scovell was the steamer's master, George Adams was clerk, John Clark was mate, William Redman and T.M. Wells were pilots, Bob Bowman was engineer, and Dave White and Ike Walcott were stewards.

Many freshmen students at Louisiana Normal arrived in Natchitoches for the first time at the train tap line at Chaplin's Lake, located near the campus of Northwestern State University.

Many residents of Natchitoches boarded trains at the Jefferson Street depot for trips that would take them throughout Louisiana.

Shown above is one of the many mule teams used to build the railroad. The first Texas and Pacific railroad bypassed Natchitoches for Cypress, but the company eventually established a railroad in Natchitoches.

These steam engines were owned by the Weaver Brothers in the early 20th century in Natchitoches Parish.

The Natchitoches City Court served as the Natchitoches Land and Railroad Company passenger depot from 1910 to 1923.

The Texas & Pacific Railroad depot, located in Natchitoches, is currently being renovated through funds from a grant by the Cane River Heritage Area. Once it is renovated, it will house a museum of African-American history.

The Texas & Pacific Railroad crew is pictured at the depot, *c.* 1905.

Eight

LOUISIANA NORMAL AND NORTHWESTERN STATE UNIVERSITY

Leopole Caspari was born in France in 1830 and immigrated to Louisiana. He lived briefly in New Orleans and settled in Cloutierville, where he started a very successful mercantile business. In 1884, he was elected to the Louisiana House of Representatives, where he served for the next four years. In 1884, he sponsored a bill establishing the Louisiana State Normal School. The school is now known as Northwestern State University. A debate arose as to the location of the school and through Representative Caspari's influence, Natchitoches was chosen as the site.

This photograph depicts the entrance to Louisiana Normal. In January 1885, the Board of Administration at Louisiana Normal hired its first maintenance person. The salary for this position was not to exceed $15 per month.

This is the old normal walk with the convent building in the background. Louisiana Normal's first president, Dr. Edward Cheib, referred to the establishment of Louisiana Normal as a half-ruined building surrounded by a wilderness of thorns and trees.

Judge Henry Adams Bullard was born in Massachusetts in 1788. He received his bachelors and masters degrees from Harvard University and he studied law in a Philadelphia law firm. Bullard joined Jose Alvarez de Toledo in his unsuccessful journey to Nacogdoches to establish an independent Texas; he was one of the few rebels to survive. He fled to Natchitoches, where he met and married Sarah Maria Kaiser. He was active in the Whig party and was elected judge, U.S. Representative, Associate Judge of the Louisiana Supreme Court, and Secretary of State of Louisiana. He later became dean of the Louisiana State Law School and was the first professor of civil law in the United States.

In 1840, Bullard Hall was donated to the Sacred Heart Order, which opened the house as a finishing school for young ladies. In the late 1870s, a yellow fever epidemic killed all of the nuns and the Sacred Heart Order decided not to reopen. It was later purchased by the citizens of Natchitoches and given to the State of Louisiana as a site for Louisiana Normal, which later became Northwestern State University.

During the Red River campaign of the Civil War in 1864, federal troops under Col. Victor Vifquin temporarily occupied Natchitoches. The colonel suspected that ammunition and perhaps Confederate troops were hiding in the Bullard mansion. However, he found none.

Three columns of the Bullard mansion remain and are the symbol of Northwestern State University. Four columns can be seen in this photograph; the fourth column was removed in the mid-1900s.

This photograph of Normal Hill was taken from Chaplin's Lake.

CONVENT BUILDING.

The Convent building was constructed for the Religious of the Sacred Heart. The sisters went to Natchitoches and established the first Catholic school in north Louisiana with six pupils in 1847. The convent building housed a chapel, assembly room, and student dormitories.

The 1902 Louisiana Normal faculty consisted of 26 professors. The president in 1902 was Beverly C. Caldwell. Male professors were paid $1250 per session while female professors were paid $750. The number of female faculty members at Louisiana Normal eventually outnumbered the male faculty members 19 to 7.

Pres. Beverly C. Caldwell introduced summer school to Louisiana Normal in 1903. Special activities were planned for the summer term, including lectures, musical entertainment, nature trips, and visits to historical places. This photograph shows the Louisiana Normal summer class of 1915.

The 1913 Louisiana Normal football team consisted of 16 players and was coached by H. Lee Prather, who was very successful. The football equipment consisted of 13 pairs of plow shoes, trousers, and cotton jerseys. The team did not have a single helmet.

The 1930 Louisiana Normal baseball team was coached by C.C. Stroud. The team played Louisiana College, Stephen F. Austin, Southwestern, and Louisiana Tech. Judge R.B. Williams, standing second on the left, played catcher and center field. Williams often said he could catch anything but could not hit worth a lick.

THE QUADRANGLE.

The Quadrangle at Louisiana Normal is shown *c.* 1924. It is believed that the buildings are the Matron's building, which was a women's dormitory; the dining hall; and East Hall, which was a men's dormitory.

VIEW FROM NORTH GATE.

This photograph shows a view from the north gate. In the background is Boyd Hall, which was an academic building. This photograph was taken *c.* 1924.

The Model School (left) was erected in 1900 under the tenure of Pres. Beverly C. Caldwell. It contained ten classrooms, four large corridors, and ten cloakrooms. Instruction at the Model School included all grades and was open to any student in the state. Guardia Hall (center) was named after Prof. Edward Guardia. The hall was one of the original buildings of the Quadrangle, and it housed the George Williamson Museum of History and the Louisiana Studies Institute's photographic collection.

The Old President's Cottage was built in 1927 during Pres. V.L. Roy's administration. The architects were Favrot and Livaudias, Ltd. of New Orleans, and the style of the cottage is Normandy French. It was the home of 10 Northwestern presidents. In the mid-1960s, a new home for the president was constructed. It is now the Alumni Center at Northwestern State University.

The Louisiana Sports Hall of Fame was founded in 1958 and its first inductees were Gaynell Tinsley, Tony Canzoneri, and Mel Ott. Since 1973, the Louisiana Sports Hall of Fame has been showcased in Prather Coliseum on the Northwestern State University campus. Each year, notable Louisiana sports figures such as Pistol Pete Maravich, Y.A. Tittle, Terry Bradshaw, Elvin Hayes, and Coach Eddie Robinson have been inducted.

The National Center for Preservation Technology and Training was created by Congress in 1992. The NCPTT is an interdisciplinary program of the National Park Service designed to advance, promote, and enhance the preservation and conservation of prehistoric and historic resources in the United States. The NCPTT is housed in the former Women's Gym on the campus of Northwestern.

114

Nine

DISTINGUISHED CITIZENS

Dr. John Sibley was a surgeon's mate in the Continental Army during the War of Independence. In September 1802, he and his family moved to Natchitoches. In March 1803, he journeyed up the Red River and made numerous contacts with the Native Americans of the Red River and Spanish Texas regions. Through correspondence with President Thomas Jefferson, he informed the president of the vast region and culture of the Indian nations, which inhabited part of the newly acquired Louisiana Purchase. In return, President Jefferson appointed Dr. Sibley surgeon to the United States Army and Indian agent to the U.S. Garrison at Fort Claiborne in Natchitoches.

Ben Deloache Johnson was born near Campti, Louisiana in 1910, to sharecropper parents. He did not receive a formal education, but at a young age displayed a knack for selling things. After training as an undertaker's assistant, he opened his first funeral home in Winnfield, Louisiana in 1930. A few years later, Johnson opened his second funeral home in Natchitoches. Through the Winnfield Funeral Home and other businesses, he became one of the most successful African-American businessmen in the United States. He has donated millions of dollars for educational endeavors.

Pierre Evariste Bossier was born in 1797 to one of the first European Creole families to settle Louisiana. His father and uncle had been soldiers in the French Army and had escaped to Louisiana to avoid political persecution. Bossier enlisted in the Louisiana militia and rose to the rank of general; he also became a very successful cotton and sugar cane planter on his plantation, Live Oaks, which rested on Cane River. A state senator and a U.S. congressman, Bossier died in office in 1844 and is buried in the Catholic Cemetery in Natchitoches.

Mayor Theodore Edward Poleman served as mayor of Natchitoches from 1920 until 1922. E.S. Cropper, a resident of Natchitoches, accused employees of the City of Natchitoches of damaging his medicinal wells. Mayor Poleman tried to appease Mr. Cropper, but Cropper refused to attend a meeting where his accusations could be addressed. On November 10, 1922, Cropper shot Mayor Poleman on Rue St. Denis. Mayor Poleman died several days later. Cropper was found guilty and spent the rest of his life in prison.

Joe Sampite served as mayor of Natchitoches from 1980 until 2000. He is married to the former Hazel Barns and is the father of four children. Sampite served in the United States Air Force during the Korean War and was a coach and teacher for 17 years at St. Mary's High School and Jesuit High School. He was president of the Louisiana Teachers Association, the Louisiana Municipal Association, and a member of the Louisiana Municipal Retirement Board. In 2000, he was inducted into the Northwestern State University Long Purple Line. Also in 2000, the *Shreveport Times* acknowledged him as one of the top 100 influential people of North Louisiana. In 2002, Sampite was inducted into the Louisiana Political Hall of Fame. During his tenure as mayor, the city of Natchitoches expanded greatly. Known for his white socks and "I Love Natchitoches" stickers, "Mayor Joe" helped Natchitoches become one of Louisiana's most popular tourist destinations.

Caroline Dormon was the first woman employed in forestry in the United States. She helped establish Kisatchie National Forest, which comprises 600,000 acres and stretches over seven parishes in North and Central Louisiana. Her family owned a tract of land named Briarwood, where Caroline Dormon resided. At Briarwood, she collected and replaced her favorite native plants. Briarwood is now a nature preserve used by conservationists and horticulturists from around the world. It is located in the sandy hills of Natchitoches Parish on Louisiana Highway 9 between Saline and Campti, Louisiana.

Lucille Mertz Hendrick served as dean of women at Louisiana Normal. She received the Outstanding Woman of the Year award from the Natchitoches Chamber of Commerce and has also been named Outstanding Tour Guide for the State of Louisiana. She is a genealogist, preservationist, and historian, and was the tour guide at Beau Fort Plantation for 12 years. Referred to as "Miss Cissy," she is known for her storytelling, charm, and Southern hospitality.

Grits Gresham is the shooting editor of *Gun and Ammo* magazine and editor-at-large of *Petersen Hunting* magazine. He is the author of seven books on hunting, fishing, and outdoor life. For more than three decades, he has served as host of several outdoor television programs, including ABC's "The American Sportsman." Gresham has written for numerous hunting, fishing, and outdoor magazines. He was a charter member of the Miller Lite All Stars and appeared in several television commercials for the company. He is also a member of the Louisiana Sports Hall of Fame.

Curtis Guillet has owned a photography studio in Natchitoches for 55 years. He has received numerous awards for photography, including first place in the prestigious Graflex Competition.

Curtis Guillet's former photography studio was located on Rue Second from 1946 until 2000. His new studio is now located on Fulton Road.

This photograph was taken by Curtis Guillet at the wedding reception of Mary Gunn and J. Bennett Johnston at Magnolia Plantation.

Curtis Guillet is a pioneer of on-location photography for product advertising. In the 1970s, he shot a series of photographs for The Service League of Natchitoches, in which he placed a variety of Louisiana food products in exterior locations. This image was taken at Beau Fort Plantation.

Robert "Bobby" Harling is the author and playwright of *Steel Magnolias*. He was instrumental in having *Steel Magnolias* filmed in Natchitoches and has a cameo appearance as the preacher in the movie.

Steel Magnolias starred Sally Field, Dolly Parton, Shirley MacLaine, Daryl Hannah, Olympia Dukakis, Tom Skerritt, Dylan McDermott, and Julia Roberts. It was filmed in Natchitoches in 1988.

THE MAN IN THE MOON

The Man In The Moon was filmed in Natchitoches Parish in 1990.

The Man In The Moon starred Sam Waterston and Tess Harper as the parents of two young girls, portrayed by Reese Witherspoon and Emily Warfield. The movie script was written by Jenny Wingfield and was based on her childhood experiences in and around Natchitoches and centered on the boy she and her sister fell in love with.

124

The first movie filmed in Natchitoches was *The Horse Soldiers*, which occurred in 1958. The movie starred John Wayne and depicted the true story of the 1,000-mile march made by Union Col. Benjamin Grierson's troops from Tennessee across Mississippi to sabotage a railroad depot that was supplying the Confederate Army at Vicksburg. The movie was directed by Bob Ford and also starred William Holden and Constance Towers.

John Gideon Lewis Sr. was born in Toronto, Canada in 1851. His family immigrated to Natchitoches in the late 19th century. He married Virginia Thompson and five children were born of the marriage. Mr. Lewis established the Prince Hall Masons of Louisiana, and Natchitoches served as the organization's home office. Mr. Lewis became Most Worshipful Grand Master of the Prince Hall Masons of Louisiana until his death, at the age of 80, in 1931.

Mary Belle DeVargas was a Natchitoches native who was born in 1902 without arms. However, her disability did not prevent her from becoming an award-winning artist. Her art studio was located on Rue Front, where the Tourist Information Center is now located. Her artwork was featured in several newspapers throughout the United States. She died in 1946.

Robert "Bobby" DeBlieux was mayor of Natchitoches from 1976 until 1980. Through his hard work, the Natchitoches Historic District was established in 1974. This photograph, taken by Curtis Guillet, reflects Bobby's sense of humor and is entitled, "A Spoof on Sensibility."

Visit us at
arcadiapublishing.com